David Royston-Lee

HOW TO WIN
FROM THE START

your number 1
CAREER
GUIDE

First published in the United Kingdom in 2010 by:
Artesian Publishing LLP
email: info@artpub.co.uk
www.artpub.co.uk

Category: Careers/Personal Development

Every effort has been made to identify and acknowledge the sources of material quoted throughout this book. The author and publisher apologise for any errors or omissions and would be grateful to be notified of corrections for any future reprint or new edition.

A CIP catalogue record for this book is available from the British Library

ISBN: 978-0-9551164-3-8

Editor: Clive Gregory

Design and typography: Anna Carson

Cartoons: Bernard Cookson

Cover: Warren Lambert & Susanne Worsfold

Printed in the UK by Wyndeham Gait

David Royston-Lee

HOW TO WIN FROM THE START

your number 1
CAREER
GUIDE

A note to readers...

For anyone new to looking for a job, it can be a really confusing and frustrating time. Everyone you talk to will give you conflicting views on 'what you need to do'! There will be many cynics who will say, 'ignore that nonsense... just get any job.' You can believe them if you wish... or you can look after number 1 by going for a number 1 job – the reality is that you might not win on the first occasion, but there is certainly no harm in trying.

At a minimum, what I can promise is that this book, if you give yourself time to do the exercises, will give you a much greater understanding of what you want out of a job – so you'll know and grasp it when you see it!

Good luck!

David

About the author

David Royston-Lee studied behavioural science at Aston University and occupational psychology at Birkbeck College, London. Having begun his career in recruitment, he became Head of Career Management Services at KPMG. David then worked as Human Resources Director of Ogilvy & Mather. He was Chief Executive of the Communication, Advertising and Marketing Foundation prior to founding Partners in Flow. As a business psychologist, David uses personal marketing to help people enhance their careers or change direction. Further information can be found at www.davidroyston-lee.com

Acknowledgements

I would like to thank those who have helped me put this book together:

- John Purkiss, my co-author on Brand You, *who helped ignite the writing fuse.*
- Peter Barber, whose expertise in publishing and calm determination pushed this book through all the production stages without any pain.
- Clive Gregory, my editor, without whom sections of this book would have remained streams of consciousness.
- Bernard Cookson, for his excellent cartoons.
- Anna Carson, for her clear typography and design.

- My wife, for her encouragement; my daughter, Alice; son, Theo; and my children's friends for their views on how people of their age would react to what I have said and how I have said it.

- And the following who have helped in a myriad of ways: Claire, Alastair & Amelia Smith; Andy & Maggie Evans; Valerie Stogdale; Oscar & Felix Wilson; Elaine Effratt; Richard Wheeler; and by no means least, Sara Cooper and James Bellini of Artesian Publishing.

There are also two other individuals who need to be mentioned:
- Sir John Hall, my ex-boss at KPMG, who encouraged me to develop my thinking on the little known, at the time, concept of 'Career Management'.
- Nella Barkley, of the Crystal-Barkley Corporation, who, after many months of exploration, served to inspire me with the Life\Work Design *process which acts as the foundation of this book.*

Lastly, I would like to thank the thousands of clients I have worked with over the last 20 years whose unique backgrounds and aspirations helped me formulate the 'tool kit' that continues to be developed. To them, I would like to say that, at last, I have put something together to answer their comment, "If only I'd known in my early 20s what I know now."

Contents

CONTENTS

A percentage of profits will be given to the Teenage Cancer Trust

INTRODUCTION | *to your number 1 career guide*

Introduction to your Number 1 Career Guide

There are many books written about jobs and work but most concentrate on the process of 'getting' a job. They are great at giving ideas and plans once you know what it is you want to do, but fall down on the crucial question:

What do I want to do?

What *do* I want to do?

So this book concentrates more on helping you to answer this sticky question and build your **own** career plan. It helps you **move** away from taking life as it comes towards being much more **in control** of what you are doing.

So if you like to take life easy, but wonder why your career isn't happening for you, or if you **actively** want to get more control over your life (OK, I admit, you won't always be in control all of the time!), start your career plan **now** by working through this book.

Building your Career Plan

The answers to the **three questions** below are crucial to planning your career:

1. Who am I?

2. Where am I going?

3. How am I going to get there?

Many career planning books concentrate on the easier questions, numbers 2 and 3. However, I will concentrate on the first question – **'Who am I?'** – with Sections B and C of this book serving to back up this fundamental aspect. This is because I believe that once you can answer 'Who am I?', the answers to the other two questions become much clearer.

The **confidence** (confidence is a crucially important characteristic for everyone) gained by going through the **analysis** phase answering 'Who am I?' allows the **exploration** phase (Where am I going?) and the **consolidation** phase (How am I going to get there?) to happen naturally.

Other books, such as *The Career Repair Kit*,[1] can help you with the more logical process of finding a job. This book helps you **balance** the **logical** process of finding a job with the **emotional** need to find something that gives you **energy**, something that you really **love** doing.

Career planning: my example

When I was leaving school I didn't know what I wanted to do.

The careers officer looked at my GCSEs and A levels and said, "What a hotchpotch... umm... let me see... yes... town and country planning!"
And for six months, I believed him....

I went to four universities for interviews, but there was something missing that I couldn't put my finger on.

This was an **important** point in my life, but how was I feeling about the four-year course at university that I decided on?

Basically, I wondered if this was right. Was everyone else **feeling** the same about their university course as me? And even if they were, and it was the norm, why did I feel extremely nervous about accepting it?

I learned later that I was at the point of 'fight or flight'. I **chose** the latter, took a year off and escaped to a kibbutz (the cool thing to do at the time!) for six months.

I didn't think about career options in Israel. I was too busy in the field picking apples or in the factory putting corn cobs, one-by-one, on a conveyor belt for eight hours a day (it took me a long time to get over the smell and actually enjoy eating them again after that!).

When I got back, however, I had changed. I was not as compliant, I knew at least what I didn't want, and started to look clearly at courses I might **like**. I picked Behavioural Science (psychology, sociology and economics). And the rest is history... well, actually it isn't.

In the final year, the 'milk round' took place and I went for 'Management Trainee' interviews with the likes of Unilever, Shell and some of the big insurance companies.

Déjà vu... I felt flat again. Was this **what** I wanted? Even after majoring in psychology and understanding personality, organisations etc, I was still unsure. Nothing excited me.

I **decided** to buck the trend and accepted a job as management trainee (their second) at a shop in Mayfair, London, ignoring comments such as, "That's not a good career decision", "What the hell did you pick that job for – what's wrong with Unilever?".

OK, you get the message. Yes, I was **stubborn**. I liked to buck the trend and my decision making was more impulsive. But I knew one thing: I was not ever going to look back on my life and say....

"If only..."

They were right. It wasn't a long term job. I **learned** a lot about retail, but ended up on the sales floor waiting for customers to come in and for someone to die so that I could get the next job up (a problem being that the oldest employee was 76... and the person whose job I wanted was only 46... I had a long time to waste!).

So, I went to the employment agency in my home town which had **helped** me with summer jobs while I was at university and they offered me a job as operations manager...

The first day, they gave me the job of interviewing new graduates. It was early summer so I actually saw a lot... Hundreds...

Déjà vu again... I found out that they didn't **know** what they wanted to do. In fact, I would say 95% of them were in the same boat that I was in at their age.

I clicked... I got really interested in understanding this and got really **passionate** about it. Some would say I found my **vocation**. Whatever it is, for the last 30 years I haven't stopped being interested in, and learning about, people and helping them find something that they might feel passionate about.

Why write a book now? I had a conversation with my daughter, Alice, and she told me what her school careers people had said when considering her options at the beginning of her A levels. I **realised** nothing has changed in 30 years! Everyone at school and university still has the same thoughts I did. Yet the world of work has got incredibly **complex** since I entered it. At that time, jobs existed for life and 50% of the **jobs** today didn't exist then.

So it was time to see if I could give some **tips**... some **exercises**... to help young people, like Alice, like you, in fact, find that passion, that 'something' that will make your working life **meaningful** to you.

That's it then... shall we get started?

WHO am I?

Who am I?

Who am I? is **the** fundamental question to answer in this book, and in life in fact, yet it is rarely addressed in schools, colleges and elsewhere.

If you have ever done some psychometric tests, you will have been answering the question, but overall such tests often serve to confuse rather than help, particularly the 'interest inventories' which I have never found helpful.

So my first tip?

Wake up!

Lots of people say: **"It took a long time for me to wake up to realising I needed a career not just a job..."**

I think it is true to say that experiencing work wakes you up to what is important to you.

So when setting out on the path to a first or new career, I recommend that you **knowingly** take a temporary job, almost any temporary job will do, just to experience what it is like!

This is part of the **exploration** process related to the second question – Where am I going? – which is **fundamental** to your success in clarifying your career. It also helps answer the **Who am I?** question.

If you can try a series of temporary jobs, working in different settings, that will help even more.

You may think the advice to take any temporary job (and I stress the *temporary* part) is odd given that the purpose of this book is to help you find the **right** career. But it's to help you **formulate** your own ideas about work and jobs based on **experience**. Many of us rely too much on others to tell us what we should be doing. I can tell you that **everyone** is an 'expert' in job search and will tell you what to do. The only problem is everyone has slightly different views and all tend to concentrate on the second two questions – where you should go, and what they think is the best way for you to do it.

Be **honest**... how many people have actually asked if you can answer the question:

Who am I?

Who am I?

Parents, teachers, friends try to help, but end up **pressurising** you to know what you want to do when you can't know... because you don't know the answer to the question.

What can make things worse is when you reply **"I don't know"**, people respond with the question...

"Well... what would you like to do?"

which is even more **frustrating**.

The easy way out is to say,

"I'll do my university course and then decide."

That keeps everyone quiet and you can escape from making any **decisions** for the next three years!

Then the pressure really is on.

You have to make a decision...

...so if you don't want to, you either **escape** and take a year off and go around the world,

...or do a Masters degree to put off the 'evil day'!

However, with the costs involved, the pressure to get a job – any job – is enormous.

...and the longer you leave it the more chance you will eventually say...

"Blow it... I'll just get any old job!"

So let's do a simple exercise to start finding the answer to **Who am I?**

The Good at/Enjoy doing grid

Hundreds of people have found this a useful **start** to managing their life and career (and, by the way, it is both **life** and **career** because they are inextricably linked).

So take a large piece of paper (preferably, flip-chart size), some **coloured** pens and draw the diagram below:

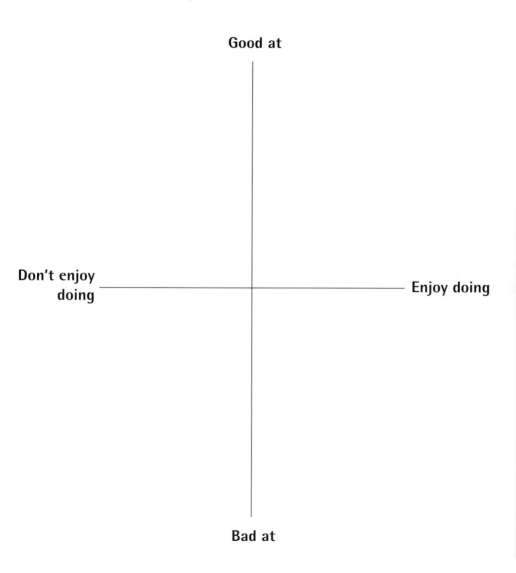

The Good at/Enjoy doing box

Start by brainstorming, or if you prefer, **thought-showering**, what you are **good at/enjoy doing**. Just jot down anything that comes into your head that you are good at and enjoy, whether to do with 'work' you have done, school activities, hobbies or life experiences. For example, your list could look something like this:

Attention to detail

Analysing ideas and turning them into something useful

Working in a team facilitating action

Presenting to small groups

Simplifying complex issues into something everyone can understand.

Then, looking outside of work, you could include:

Fixing things... people... plans... ideas

Playing the guitar

Helping sort out problems with my friends

Listening hard and understanding issues.

When you have exhausted your thoughts, **ask** others around you what they see as things you are good at and seem to enjoy. If you disagree, discuss with them until you identify words or phrases you can include in that box.

I've already mentioned that we get pressure from others to make decisions, so why am I suggesting you get **feedback** from them?

Because this is different – you are asking for **specific information** about you... and it helps you to be more aware of yourself from an external perspective.

One useful model to consider at this stage is the Johari Window – our objective at understanding 'Who I am' is to know as much as we can about the window on ourselves.

The Johari Window

The model came from two Americans, Joe and Harry, who explained that we often have 'blind spots' – things about ourselves that we are not aware of, but that others see. The more we are aware of what others see in ourselves, the more line 'a' moves to the right. The more it moves, the more we are aware of both our 'blind spots' and how our subconscious is controlling our lives.

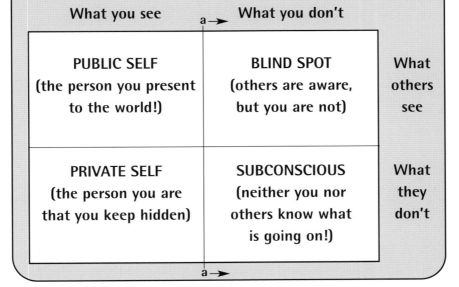

(adapted by David Royston-Lee 2010)

Luft J, Ingham H (1955) *The Johari window, a graphic model of interpersonal awareness*, proceedings of the Western Training Laboratory in Group Development (Los Angeles: UCLA)

After feedback about what others think, you might add to your grid:

Telling jokes to ease situations

Motivating others by encouraging action

Being there for my friends.

So you have at least 15 words and phrases that you have included in the **Good at /Enjoy doing** box. The next stage is to populate the other boxes...

The Good at/Don't enjoy box

The **Good at/Don't enjoy** box contains what you are good at, but actually have little or no interest in.

This box reveals things that may have interested you once, but that you don't enjoy any more. Some people might say you should continue to do more when you ask them. But you know that you've been there and earned the T shirt so many times that it is now boring – and you have had enough.

So your examples could include...

Cross-country running

Playing the clarinet

Cleaning up(!)

Tidying my room

...washing...

If you continue doing those things you don't enjoy, you will cut corners, leave doing them to the last minute and eventually, if you are not careful, those activities will drop into the box below. (OK, there are some things like **washing** that you have to do if you want others to stay around you!).

A thought...

Don't get caught up with the "Shoulds" and "Oughts". In the long run, they don't make us happy.

Example: A client of mine took mathematics at university because he was good at it, and his parents told him he had to use this talent and go on to accounting, which he did . At 35 he came to me extremely unhappy. Yes, he was 'successful' in his parents and other people's eyes, but he hated accountancy. Enough said, at this moment...

The Don't enjoy/Bad at box

The **Don't enjoy/Bad at** box contains three sub-boxes:

   1) those things you just simply don't want to do

   2) those things you know you are not good at, and

   3) those things you think you are not good at, but have not tried.

Examples for each sub-box could be:

   1. Bungee-jumping... accounts... cold-calling... flower arranging...

   2. Arguing... physical conflict... football... being on time... cooking without recipes

   3. Sculpture... singing... graphic design... teaching/training...

The Enjoy doing/Bad at box

Now the last box... the interesting one entitled **Enjoy doing/Bad at**. Enter here everything you've always wanted to do or try, but never had the **time** to do; things you're interested in but have always fallen short of actually doing anything about... things not at the top of your priority list.

This box is important because it will help avoid saying **"If only"** later on in your life – the so-called 'missed opportunities'. Now is the time to do something about them.

So just think about, and put down on paper, those things you'd like to do... those things you'd like to try. Brainstorm all those things you'd like to put in that box.

Examples could be:

Learn the piano

Take up horse-riding

Explore the media world

Do a creative writing course

Try scuba diving.

Once the four boxes are filled, put the exercise aside and revisit it once or twice over a week to see if you can add other words or phrases. Then ask your friends, family and work colleagues to have a look and add any others that crop up (remembering the Johari Window!).

Note that this isn't a task, it is a **process**. In other words, it is not the writing down that is important, it is the **thinking** about who you are and your life that matters. Hence why it's good to revisit the chart on more than one occasion, and ask friends, family and work colleagues to help you complete it.

Delving deeper

The next stage is to start asking yourself **Why?**, to delve **deeper** into each word and phrase.

So in terms of the examples I have for the **Good at/Enjoy doing** box, what specifically is underneath each of those words and phrases that would describe **me** more accurately?

Well, **Attention to detail** means for me:

>   1) Needing to understand fully anything I put my mind to
>
>   2) Ensuring I get things right
>
>   3) Soaking up everything around the subject of my attention and seeing how things 'fit'.

'**Analysing ideas and turning them into something useful**' is already quite expansive compared to just **Analysing**, but may also mean other things as well. There may be similar but slightly different underlying needs... so I might...

>   1) Like to put a blueprint of analysis over everything I do
>
>   2) Like to make things 'safe' in everyone else's eyes
>
>   3) Like to make sure that I am not wrong and in control.

Here, I have asked the question **Why**? after each statement to go down three levels to understand 'what's in it for me' to enjoy and be good at '**Analysing**'.

So, my friends and acquaintances might say about me: "Oh, David's very analytical about what he does." That is correct, but represents just an **on-the-surface** picture. When I ask myself, "Why am I analytical?", I get to the third level answer that gives the real reason... it's so that "I am not wrong and that I am in control." This gives me a deeper **understanding** of the underlying need (to not be wrong) to one of the entries in my Good at/enjoy doing box.

It is important to recognise that the **reason** we do something has a **deeper** cause than that apparent on the surface.

I suggest you do this with as many of the points you have put in the top right-hand box as possible and then look at the other boxes to see what may be underpinning some of the things you do not want to do or 'think' you are bad at.

Hopefully, as you do this exercise, certain **themes** will arise and there will be similar third-level reasons why you enjoy something and are good at it.

For example, already you may have noticed something above about **getting things right**, something about **creating a pattern** that is **safe** and being **in control**...

These themes may well be important underlying factors in anything you do and have an important part to play when we look at your **Purpose** later.

If we look at the examples from the other boxes, I don't like to be in a situation where I cannot control the outcome. Football relies on a team to win; and I don't like being controlled by others – hence the problem with being on time!

I don't like cooking without a recipe because leaving it to chance, for me, is unsafe. In terms of things I'd like to do, piano is safe (I am in control) and the same might apply to, for example, learning a new language (it's all up to me). The horse riding shows I can control something apart from myself, but I still know that, with practice, I can be in **control**.

From the above we are getting a picture of **me** just by looking at the answers and can see that certain areas of work would be interesting for me to **explore** when considering career opportunities, while there are others that may be best avoided.

If the themes are strong, they are important to note because all the research done into how we operate points to one **truth** — we don't change that much. The way we operate can be modified, but we don't normally change radically. We might pretend to change by **re-labelling** what we do, but totally changing behaviour doesn't tend to happen.

This is why developing a greater understanding of who you are is important. You may look at others and wish you were more like them, but if it is not in your make-up, it will never happen.

Most of us know very little about our own capabilities. I tend to think of us as being like an **iceberg** with only a small percentage of our ability **visible** to us and other people – and sometimes other people know us more than we know ourselves...

So your **mission** (*should you choose to accept it!*) is to complete this first exercise...

If you can't get down to doing it all, it just may not be the right time for you to do this at the moment... you should only do this if you have the energy – the 'oomph' – to do it.

Understanding yourself even more

A way to understand yourself even more is to use the concept of **Detached Involvement** created by Jagdish Parikh in his excellent book *Managing Your Self: Management by Detached Involvement.*[2] Dr Parikh's view is that you need to detach yourself from your situation to truly see what your situation is.

When you are in whatever your situation is, you cannot see it clearly. It is just like when you are sitting in a chair; the chair **supports** you, it may or may not be comfortable, but the weight of you in it means it is difficult to move, and it may be difficult to see behind you as the chair is facing one way. Only by getting out of the chair can you walk around it and also **move** it. Only by getting yourself temporarily out of your situation can you take a walk around it and get a full view of it.

By using Dr Parikh's idea, you get the ability to see yourself in **action**, almost like you are seeing yourself from the corner of a room, or hovering above yourself... if you can get into this state it is much easier to 'examine yourself' and clearly answer **Who am I?**

Use the following two **tools** to help:

Push yourself 'out of kilter'

By changing something to make you feel physically uncomfortable, you will become more aware of your situation and the way you operate.

The change can be quite simple. It just needs to be something that you will **notice**. Examples include:

+ Moving your watch to your other wrist;
+ Keeping a notepad and pen in your pocket all the time. It should be big enough to feel uncomfortable... The beauty of the pad and pen is that if anything comes into your head that you want to **remember**, you can jot it down while in this 'detached yet involved' state;
+ Wearing different nail varnish from your normal colour.

You can also **change** the clothes you wear; the time you get out of bed; what you do when you get up in the morning. As long as you break the routines you are used to, you will notice what you are doing in a detached, yet involved, way.

Three hugs a day

It is also useful to understand how you are **feeling** – particularly if you are a more practical person, if you are a 'do-er' more than a 'thinker'.

Using a scale of 1-10 where **1** is suicidal (well, feeling pretty lousy), **5** is boringly normal and **10** is ecstatic, write down three times a day the number that reflects how you are feeling.

Preferably make this note when you get up in the morning, sometime around midday and then before you go to bed. So in that little note pad you've bought, you will have three numbers for each day.

And each time you write down a number, write next to it an answer to the question:

What can I do to make me feel one point better?

That is not to say you will do it... the point is to notice how **you** can make yourself feel a little better.

We do not change that much throughout our life. The changes we can make that last tend to be small steps... the smaller the step, the easier it is to take.

So you might feel a **3**... which often means reasonably depressed and lethargic... having difficulty getting up in the morning... and waking up in the night worried.

To change your situation up one point, you might know that you feel much better if you force yourself up by a certain time and go to the gym... or for a run... or give help and support to someone else.

If you do this for a week, you will find something happens. You will become much more aware of what you can do to get yourself into gear... isn't it always the case when you are feeling a bit low that you blame everyone else? The classic 'blame' at the moment is "Because of the credit crunch there are no jobs... so I won't even bother looking." As my daughter said... **"yeah... right!!"** (She is working for a catering company when she is not at uni... so there are jobs for those who look).

Sometimes all we need is a bit of **Oomph**... we need to take control of our lives rather than believe the world out there controls us.

...and why is it called 'three hugs a day'?

Because it was named that by one of my clients who believed it was a great way to look after herself. She said it was like giving herself three hugs a day.

And even more still...

OK, so you're still with me. You've understood a bit more about **Who am I?** and have got some underlying themes.

You have also developed a little 'detached involvement', have 'knocked yourself out of kilter' and you are more aware of what you can do to make yourself feel a little better using the 'three hugs' exercise.

The next stage is to **examine** what you have actually done in your life to date.

Your personal kit bag

Most of us have a metaphorical kit bag on our back from the moment we are born. While we run through life, we throw all of our experiences, talents, fascinations, interests, plans and ideas into it.

Take a look inside *your* kit bag now!

WHO AM I?

Now is the time to **stop**... take your kit bag off... empty it on the ground and have a good **rummage** through it!

We want to go one stage further than the Good at/Enjoy doing grid and actually understand ourselves by looking at the **past**, not just the **present**, in light of what we want out of our **future**.

We might not know yet what we do **want** out of the **future**. Our past, however, can give us some ideas.

Having a really good **look** at what we have done in our lives to date will **inform** us in terms of what we can do in the **future**.

The next exercise is the most important one. It is useful to do now and to continue to update as you travel through your life. This exercise is also useful for deciding what we want to keep **hold** of... what we want to **throw away**... what we want to **develop**... in terms of our talents and also what we want to **add** to the things in our kit bag (those thoughts we might have in terms of the results of the exercise 'Enjoy doing/Bad at', for example).

It's important to **realise** that there might be a lot of **stuff** in your kit bag that is just holding you back, and weighing you down.

> A thought... on 'stuff'
>
> It is amazing how much 'stuff' we have to do every day. All the things that need doing, but get in the way of what we really want to do. We can become so weighed down with 'things that need doing' that we never have time for the things that will move us on in our lives...

Your Life Line

What you need to do is **re-evaluate** what you have, and what you want to have more of as you move into the future.

So take another piece of flip-chart paper (or tape 6 pieces of A4 together. As my daughter points out, no student has access to flip-chart paper) and draw 'My life line' to look like this:

Your Life Line

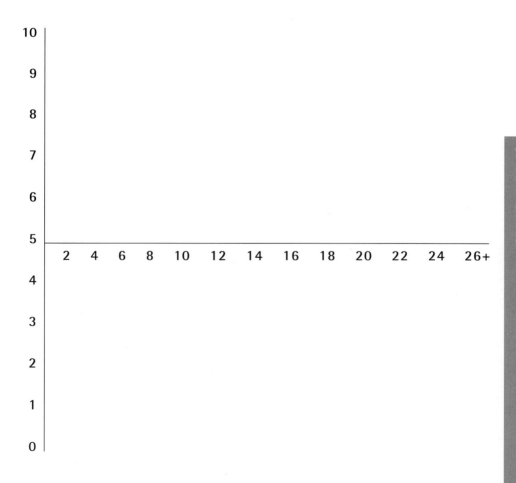

The same scale is on the vertical axis you used before (where 0 equals suicidal and 10 equals ecstatic with 5 being boringly normal). Along the horizontal axis are the years of your life broken up into two-year chunks.

OK... so next in the exercise is to note all the **high points** in your life to date.

The purpose of this exercise is to remember as many 'high points' in your life to the present time as you can.

High points are simply those times we remember as pleasurable times, where we felt some satisfaction, pride... gratitude that we were there, or a sense of achievement.

What we tend to remember better are the **low points.** So we are trying to create more **balance**.

It is fine to jot low points down too, as they often remind us of the good times that came before or after!

However, we do not want to spend too much time on them because all of us remember bad news much more than good (in fact, bad news carries seven times more weight than good news!)

So, let's try to concentrate on good news and only consider the bad when it happens to coincide with the good... for example, in those situations when you thought you'd get bad news but the opposite was true. Or you were petrified of doing something new... only to find that you enjoyed it!

Real high points

Try not to put things down that are important to other people... rather, concentrate on those **real** high points for you.

There are many people I see who are great at passing exams with top marks... it is like getting out of bed in the morning for them!

So they may only put getting an A grade at A-level as a 5 or possibly a 6.

They might remember with much more excitement going fishing with their dad; winning a swimming prize; learning to ride their bicycle... or making their first real friend... that holiday with mates from school... the first concert... or first boy/girlfriend.

Check with yourself and put down the things that have an emotional **meaning**, not just things that 'logically' should be there (this is why the scaling exercise we discussed is important) to make sure you are not simply putting down as highs, those events or times that were highs common to everyone.

The reason for the focus on your highs is that we want to identify the **uniqueness** of you, because high points are normally when you are **in flow** – when you are using your talents in the right way, in the right environment, with the right kind of people.

It is also important to look at **gaps** in your Life Line... because, let's face it, if you can't think of any highs over a year, you must be a pretty sad person! If you can't **remember** what was happening at a particular time in your life, ask those who may know to remind you what you were doing... it is often surprising what you have **forgotten**.

So again... check with parents, siblings, friends etc. It is amazing how a short discussion can open a window onto a particular period of your life.

It is important to gather information from others because at whatever time you look back over your life, you will be looking from the 'comfort zone' of whatever situation you are in at the time... and will only see what is relevant to you at that particular time.

This relates back to why you need to get detached from your situation – because it is only when you can see yourself from the point of detachment that you will be able to change.

Your first 10 years

Once you have identified the high points using the above methods thoroughly, look particularly at the highs in your first 10 years.

This is a **critical** time. It is the time before the external world has imposed itself on what you do, the time before teachers and parents started to tell you what you were good at or **should** be good at! The external world starts to look for 'brilliance' but forgets that you might not **enjoy** a particular subject...

So complete the first 10 years as well as you can and then ask yourself, "So, what was I doing? What talents were there? And looking through my life to date, what talents were developed from that time?"

Write all the talents you can see on the bottom of the 'Life Line' chart... Can you see themes emerging across the high points?

Can you see that you have tended to use certain talents in particular ways, in particular environments with particular people?

Now it is important to get a little organised and identify themes in terms of...

    1) The **talents** you use
    2) **Where** you use them
    3) **With whom**.

When you have done that, check your thoughts in terms of themes with those around you... do they agree? Do they see the same themes in you?

What you could do as a quick test before sharing your thoughts is to first ask others what they would say about you to someone else... both good and bad. Literally... if you do this with five people, some themes will emerge.

Try it!

Now identify the five key high points... the ones which score more highly. Are there any **extra elements** at those times that made them even more memorable, exciting, interesting or enjoyable?

Then take out your Good at/Enjoy doing grid... How do the themes that are emerging link with what you found on that?

Now we need to do some consolidation....

The Post-It™ note exercise

Sharing 'stories' with others is an important way of getting attuned to talking about yourself. I was introduced to this particular method by Nella Barkley of the Crystal-Barkley Corporation.[3]

Most of us are extremely bad at doing this... I help many people who had all the talents and skills for a job, but who failed at the interview stage because they were hopeless in terms of understanding their talents... and even worse at expressing them!

This is a thing we are not taught at school... how to **talk** about ourselves clearly so people know exactly who we are and what we can do.

The main problem is we are taught to think in terms of 'teams'. Therefore, when we talk about times that were good, we have a tendency to give a history lesson of what **WE** did... not what **I** did.

It's an illness actually... lots of people I see suffer from **I** trouble!!

So look at the five key high points and go through what **you** did... what was **your** role in that situation? What did **you** do that you felt proud of? What were **your** achievements and what did they lead on to?

Practise each story with someone who will keep checking you are saying 'I' instead of 'We'!

So... buy some Post-It™ notes and identify people who:

> • were **involved** in the situations you will talk about
> • **know you** well in a work or outside work context
> • **don't know you** that well at all.

You will need about 10 minutes with each person individually or 25+ minutes if you are telling a story to more than one person. (It's actually better if you have a small group).

Give them all a batch of sticky notes and ask them to listen to your story and write down each talent they **hear** on a separate note.

When they give the notes back to you, ask them to explain what they have 'seen'. Your story should normally take 3-4 minutes... and give time at the end for people to ask **questions to clarify** talents.

You will know if you are doing this exercise correctly by the number of completed notes you receive! If you only get one or two, you will be giving a history lesson about 'what **we** did' rather than 'what **I** did'....

As you tell the story to different people subsequently, you will find that you will become more eloquent about your talents and will receive more completed notes back... it is something that gets better with practice!

One thing to note as you do this is that it is always amazing to find out that some people have a talent for listening and giving great feedback... and some are hopeless!

When you receive the completed notes, **check** what's been written and if you are not sure about what is on a note, ask for further explanation and add to what is written so that it makes sense to you.

So if you received a note saying 'Achievement'... what does that mean? How does your friend see that word reflected in you and where?

It would be good to make sure that, on each note, you get:

> 1) A talent
> 2) How you used it
> 3) Where you used it.

Yes, it does take a bit of time, but it is really worth it!

This will all feel incredibly **uncomfortable** at first... naturally... because it is one of those things that gets you out of your comfort zone... and you are asking others for help... and it is talking about yourself... and it could be embarrassing... I'm sure that many people would say talking about themselves is in the Don't enjoy/Bad at box!

By doing this exercise of sharing stories with others a number of things happen, all of which benefit you.

    1) You **learn to talk** about yourself...

    2) You get **feedback** on your talents, how you use them and where...

    3) You build **confidence**, particularly when different people all give you similar positive feedback that you can't ignore...

    4) With feedback you **get better** at talking about yourself and become more articulate...

    5) And the most important thing in any subsequent interview is the **ability to talk** about your talents, know how you use them and where, giving examples.

As your key talents emerge from this exercise, you can also see other times where you use them, so that the number of stories has a tendency to grow.

Just doing this exercise will put you head and shoulders above 75% of the population in the success-at-interview situation.

So collect those sticky notes like **gifts** and collect as many as possible. You will find that the more times you tell your stories (and to different people), the better the results. OK, some people don't have a talent for 'spotting' talents and others will be brilliant at it – we can't all be brilliant at everything!

Be persistent and you will benefit enormously. You'll find talents you never thought you had and see how valuable they can be in differing situations... and, interestingly, as you tell stories to others, they will also make suggestions where you might want to explore career choices.

When you have done this exercise with at least 10 to 15 people, you will have a lot of Post-it™ notes. Try to get at least 100... then you can start to look at them and group them again into themes.

What do the notes say about how you relate to others?

What talents seem to be the ones everyone recognises?

In what situation are you at your best?

When do you work on your own and when with groups?

What do I mean by 'talents'- rather than 'skills'?

Talents are those things you were born with that you were able to develop easily. Skills are learned, but are not 'natural' to you. That doesn't mean you might not enjoy the skill immensely, but unless there is an underlying talent, something will be missing – that passion, that thing some people call **'Oomph'** without which it is not 'complete'. Talents are deep-rooted and tend, if developed, to end up being used again and again and constantly improved upon. Expertise is based on inherent talent.

What we have done so far...

I think it is time to take a breather for a moment and reflect on what we (you!) have done so far...

- We have looked at what your **thoughts** are at the present time... the Good at/Enjoy doing grid... and delved deeper into this to understand what is, in effect, driving you at the moment

- We've looked at trying to detach ourselves from our present situation to **see ourselves** more clearly... and knocked ourselves out of kilter while giving ourselves some hugs each day!

- Then we have got to **know ourselves** more – this time looking at the past and the kit bag of experiences we have collected in our journey through life so far

- We've looked in detail at our **high points**, extracted talents from them and checked them out. We've refined how we use them, and in what situations, through the Post-it™ note exercise.

So... we have looked at the **present**... and the **past**.... now we need to look at the **future** a little bit ... even though it may still be pretty hazy.

We need to look at the future from the point of view of 'our purpose'. This gives us our compass on the journey through the rest of our life... without dictating exactly what we might do next.

Your purpose

What is your **purpose**? This is the million dollar question!

Some people spend their whole life looking for purpose – like the priest in Rudyard Kipling's book *Kim*[4], always searching for a particular river which he only finds with his death, not realising that, in fact, his purpose was **the journey**.

So how do you find yours?

Let's begin with the following diagram.

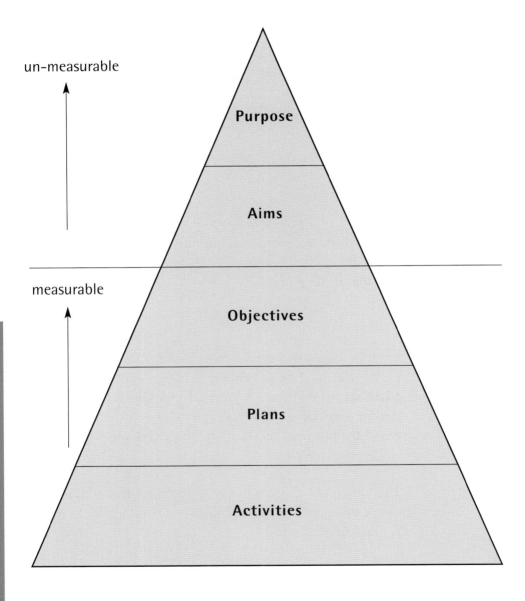

un-measurable

measurable

Purpose

Aims

Objectives

Plans

Activities

Let's start at the bottom and work up...

We spend 95% of our time doing **tasks and activities**.... rushing through life, running from doing one activity to another... lots of 'stuff'.

WHO *am I?* **A**

Next we have **plans**, what we want to do next weekend... next month... for the next holiday, etc.

We have **goals and objectives** beyond plans, both short and long term... such as getting a good job; a better one; a car; a home; a lover/spouse, etc...

All of these are measurable... as time goes on, we can measure quite clearly if we have been able to achieve each of them...

And when we achieve our goals and objectives... we will set **new** ones... just bigger and better... and so life goes on... reaching goals and then setting new ones.

Most people **live** their lives going from one goal to the next; one plan to the next and one activity to the next, and live reasonable lives striving for the next goal... that is fair enough...

BUT...

All of us have those moments when we talk about the fact there must be more to life... we talk about **something** missing... wanting something **meaningful**, something that's a bit more exciting, something that drives us from the **centre** of ourselves rather than some external force like the needs of the organisation we work for... something more than a sales target or the next pay rise.

If we understand that, we can move into the un-measurable 'zone' and rather than work **up** to goals... work **down** from purpose. Our lives will then have so much more meaning.

Why?

Because we know **why** we are doing what we are doing!

Abraham Maslow[5] (1908-70), a psychologist whose work has been prominent throughout many decades, has a lot to answer for... look at the following diagram:

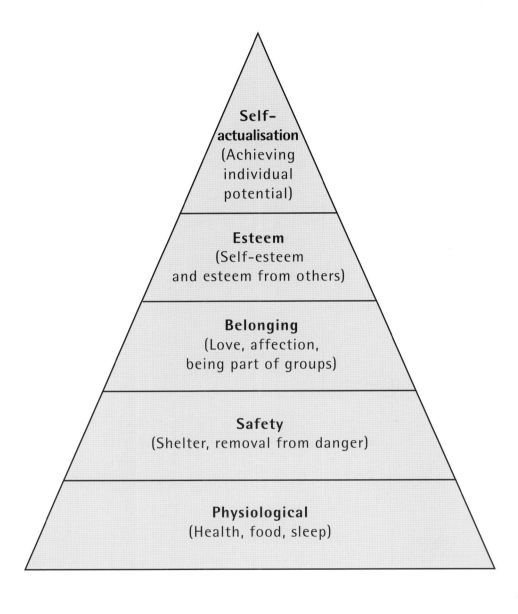

You'll notice it is quite similar to the purpose triangle....but in some ways it is very different.

Even today we look at Abraham Maslow's 'Hierarchy of needs' as a way of understanding human motivation. Go on any management course and when you look at **managing** people, Maslow is bound to come up.

He talked about human **needs** that, once satisfied, allow people to move on to higher level needs culminating in something he called "Self-actualisation".

So at the basic level, the 'Physiological' one – our need is for food and water.

Once we have this, we look for shelter and safety...

Once this is satisfied, we move to finding love – another human being to share our life with...

And in work, after that, we look for respect and esteem.

Eventually, we reach, in Maslow's terms, a state of self-actualisation where we are happy, with all our needs satisfied, having achieved our potential.

Except that I don't believe that this model works in today's society.

Things have changed...

So going back to the purpose diagram – Maslow's theory goes as far as objectives... but no further. The journey he proposes, where we have to go through distinct need states and only find 'self-actualisation' (in our words – **purpose**) after we have worked through lower order needs, is not acceptable. Why should we wait?

Wouldn't it be better to understand what 'self-actualisation' looks like before we embark on our **journey** through life?

So my proposal is to turn Maslow's theory on its head and start with finding what 'self actualisation' looks like... the quest to find our purpose.

We have completed lots of exercises that can help us find the clues to this...

- What about the themes in the **Good at/Enjoy doing** exercise?

- What are the talents in the top right hand box that we **cannot stop using?**

- What are the underlying themes that run through our **Life Line**, like words through a stick of seaside rock?

- Which **words** do our friends use to describe us to others?

In other words, what are those aspects of us that are **un-measurable?**

What are the things we **cannot stop doing?**

I see people who, given a financial problem, will work on it, forgetting time and everything else on their 'to-do' list... they are totally immersed in solving the problem...

Or the secretary, who in a **crisis** everyone will turn to for help, bypassing the human resources department and the employee assistance programme...

Or the old man of 90 who goes up on the roof of his neighbour's house if there is a loose tile...

I believe we all have certain aspects of us that are like an **itch**... they need constant scratching!!

Why?

Because the more we use the talents that **drive us**... the more we want to use them.

And the more we want to use them, the more we realise we need to **learn**

more, train more, go to the next level... and the more our appetite becomes **insatiable**. In effect, the more we become addicted to doing certain things, in certain ways with certain people... when we become aware that there are certain things we do in certain ways that **energise** us... then we have broken through the ceiling above 'goals/objectives' into the area of our aims, our insatiable aims which are **never satisfied** and therefore cannot be measured.

These **aims** have something to do with our purpose... and actually we don't need to know exactly what they have to do with our purpose to accept them.

Once we are aware of our aims, whatever life throws at us, however many crossroads we reach along the way, we have an **internal compass** that tells us which route to follow.

So we work from our underlying purpose (which might take a lifetime... and probably will... to understand) to our more visible aims – knowing what it is that we cannot stop doing, translating those aims into the measurable realm... of **realistic**, measurable goals and objectives.

From that point on we have some idea **why** we are on the journey we are on... what we want to achieve in terms of our plans and, interestingly, on a day to day basis, we know how to prioritise our tasks and activities... why?... because there is **meaning** to them...

We know why we are doing what we are doing.

There is a **reason** why we are doing what we are doing. And it doesn't matter what title we have in work, what market we are in, what role we take, as long as it fulfils our 'purpose'.

It is important to say here that some people find it quite **frightening** to have a purpose – they are scared that their world will become narrow in some way.

This is far from the truth in that finding aspects of your purpose actually opens so many **more opportunities** than you ever felt possible.

Focus on what you do rather than what you might be...

We need to understand the difference between being 'role' focused and 'purpose' focused.

Confused?

It goes back to how we are taught to look at the world, particularly the world of work...

From a young age we are asked what we want to **be** – with the expected response... "a doctor, a train driver, a nurse, a millionaire!"

When you look at job titles you have no idea, actually, what the job entails.

We don't know that being a nurse can mean a **multitude** of talents being used in a myriad different ways... for example, not all nurses or doctors look after patients.

I often hear the comment, "I don't want to be a boring banker", normally from people who don't have the first clue what banking is all about.

When I worked in advertising, lots of people wanted to work in what they thought was a sexy and cool environment... but when interviewed, had **no idea** about what working in advertising was all about.

You need to get **detached** from all the jobs out there and the perceptions that have been created around them.

You need to look at what really goes on, what people actually do... you will see that there are a lot of different talents needed that are similar in different roles.

Bankers need to build good relationships with their clients, just as doctors do... the **difference** lies in what drives us. What attracts us to either role has a lot to do with our underlying needs as a person... our purpose.

We need to identify our purpose in terms of **how** we want to use our talents.

This means understanding more about **Who I am**.

To understand more about how we use our talents and help us get closer to understanding our purpose, we need a clearer understanding of our **values**... then we will realise why we might prefer to **explore** nursing rather than banking... engineering rather than architecture... construction rather than catering... and also see that making snap judgements on differing roles may be extremely **unproductive** in the long run.

Your Values

Values tend to get dismissed in the **busy-ness** of our day to day lives... yet values affect everything we do and force us to question the direction in which we are heading.

Values are closely linked with your belief system and help you to make the right decisions in your life. They control and guide any decisions you make... whether at home or at work.

Also, if they are compromised too much, they can lead to physical and mental illness... so values are pretty important!

The following exercise is to help you understand your values.

The Admirations Exercise*

Get a lined sheet of paper again and draw a line down the middle like this:

People I admire	Why I admire them

*adapted from the Crystal-Barkley *Life\Work Design* Program

What you need to do first is write down all the **people** you admire.

Why use the word **admire** rather than another, such as **respect**?

Because respect is a stronger word. If you admire someone, you may not respect them... they might have qualities that may dismiss them from the list. It is a small difference but hopefully you can see that you might **include** more people in your list whom you might not like or respect... but actually have a secret admiration for!

Again, as before, brainstorm your thoughts onto the paper. Just start writing your list and keep going. If you are having trouble thinking of **people**, you are probably thinking too much!

You might be **thinking** why you might not put them on the list... in other words, you are putting the bar too high.

Don't think too much, that always stops creative brainstorming... try to just go with your **intuition**.

It doesn't take one shot or two... you need to think about this exercise over a few days adding to it as you come up with names. As I have said, including people on your list doesn't mean they are perfect in every way – they may have only one redeeming feature, but if they come into your mind, write them down.

Some helpful hints are:

Start thinking of those close to you. Family, friends... teachers who **inspired** you at school and college, those you have been close to in the past.

Then look outside that to people in your local community that attract you in some way.... and go beyond that to those in the public eye that you admire ... sports personalities, musicians, film stars, political figures.

Then look at figures from history such as great thinkers, writers, artists, heroes, outlaws and so on...

Think about whom you admire and why

Write the list first and try to get to at least 20 people... more than that is even **better**!

The next stage is to write down **all** the reasons **why** you admire them in each case.

If the same qualities/reasons keep coming up, keep putting them down and try to be specific.

So, for instance, if **courage** comes up – courage in what circumstances?

How were they courageous... was it split second or over time?

Were the circumstances life threatening, or was it that they simply kept going in the face of ridicule?

Then do the same exercise... but this time... look at **things** you admire
You may find this more difficult than doing the people exercise... or vice-versa.

'Things' are anything other than people that affect you positively in some way, make you stop, remind you of something pleasurable...

On this list you may have the **smell** of a particular dish cooking, or of an old book, the aroma of freshly cut grass, the sea, a rose...

Or you may be reminded of a place that you **see** in your mind's eye... that exhilarating storm, for example.

It may be something you **hear**... like a particular song that has meaning for you...

It may also have to do with a **feeling** it evokes in you... for example, walking into an old church may bring a sense of calm (and the smell may also evoke this feeling too!)

Things I admire	Why I admire them

For others, it is to do with being inspired to **think**... some technology that makes you think **Wow!** For instance, having a **fascination** with mobile phones, jumbo jets, computers... for others, it's architecture or design or art or writing or science.

What are the reasons for these things **grabbing** you in some way?

Then, lastly, look at doing the same exercise with **groups** of people...

This simply means looking at groups of two or more people who have come together for whatever **cause**.

So, you might include any group from Muse to Iron Maiden, from Amnesty International to a political party, from racing drivers to your local firemen.... or your local hospice volunteers to Save the Children.

Keep going... keep adding until you know you can't add any more (for some reason, this tends to be more difficult than the other two, although it is interesting that everyone is able to complete one of the three easily and has problems with the others).

Again, write down **all** the qualities that you admire in each of your groups. If the same quality/reason keeps coming up, keep putting it down remembering to be as **specific** as you can...

Once all have been completed, look across all the qualities you have given.

Which keep occurring?

What words spring out at you from each of the exercises?

Can you see links across the exercises?

Now try to identify the **top** 10 qualities that either come up the most... or **resonate** with you the most...

Groups I admire	Why I admire them

Write them down... and if there is an order to them, put them in that order so you can see which are most **meaningful** to you.

The top 10 represent **your values**... the positive qualities you see in other people that are the qualities you are trying to emulate.

So again... get detached and look at the lists you created... what do they say about you overall?

Does this exercise also link with some of the other exercises in terms of clarifying what drives you... what excites you... what you can't stop doing... does it **clarify**, a little more, your purpose?

Look at your Life Line and see how your values may have affected choices in the past ... and how the things you are good at and enjoy are linked strongly with the values you have come up with, in terms of how you use your talents.

Another exercise that overlaps with this one and looks at Who am I? from a different perspective is the Environments Exercise.

Your Environment

We often forget that the environment we find ourselves in affects our ability to operate at our **optimum**.

Get to know which working environment suits you best

If we think back over our lives, normally we have a perception of which environments are more conducive to particular activities... we know that we revised for exams best in certain physical circumstances with access to certain people and with a certain amount of control over our situation.

For instance, some people know they get distracted easily by their possessions around them, so prefer to go to a library rather than work in their room. Others know that they work better in the mornings, or late at night...

Some learn best through listening and discussing with others... while others prefer to read books...

I'm writing this book in an apartment in Nice, in April... why?

Because I'm cut off from every distraction at home... I prefer to work alone... I have to go to the internet café if I want to get online... also I feel better when it is sunny and work harder for some reason if it is warm outside... I have French music radio on... which gives a beat that somehow stimulates me to type quicker!!

Crazy? Or is it? I know it works for me.

So what about you?

What is your preferred environment... where and when are you are at your most productive?

The Environments Exercise*

So for this exercise... another sheet of paper. Let's start with your **Physical** environment...

My Physical Environment

Toxic	Nutritious

*adapted from the *Crystal-Barkley Life\Work Design* Program

WHO AM I?

Look back at some of the previous exercises... the **Life Line** in particular, what needs to be in your physical environment for you to be firing on all cylinders?

What physical environments stop you from being energised?

I've used the words 'toxic' and 'nutritious' to express how you might feel at the extremes... in other words what environments 'poison' you and which ones 'feed' you?

For example, I find working in close proximity with people who are on the phone extremely distracting from the noise point of view... I need lots of light... I hate working in a windowless office... I don't like strong or stale food smells... I love to be able to walk out into a garden... or park... I love the bustle of a city...

Now let's look at the amount of **control** you need in your environment. This is about how much you are in control and how you feel if some of your responsibility is taken away from you. Some of us like to be told what to do and we get on with it... we stop when the job is done and do not think beyond the task in hand.

For example, if your parents ask you to cut the grass, you will probably do it... but not get rid of the grass cuttings... you won't cut the edges of the lawn... won't see other things that might need doing in the garden... because you were **not asked** to do it.

Other people would prefer someone to say **"Look after the garden..."** and they will take pleasure in doing what they think is important to do.

Look at how you prefer to work. Do you like others having some control over you... some guidelines, like a job description?

Do you prefer a **culture** of hard work and late nights in a team where everyone is **focused** on getting something done by a deadline, or do you prefer to work hard on your own and to be able to leave by 6pm?

Control in my Environment

Toxic	Nutritious

Or do you like a culture of winner-takes-all versus working as a team? Do you like the pressure of mistakes not being tolerated versus learning by mistakes?

Lastly, look at environments from a **people** perspective.

Write the aspects of people that you find difficult to stomach and aspects that help you to do your best... those which energise you.

An easy way to do this is to think of walking down your local street....You see someone walking towards you in the distance... what is it about that person that will make you quicken your step... or decide to cross the road to avoid them?

Look at the results of this exercise. Does it clarify what it is important to have in your environment and what it is best to avoid?

Ask yourself what environments are more **conducive** to your way of operating – which support you more and **enable** you to work to your maximum potential?

You may not think this is important, but I can assure you I see lots of people who were attracted to the right job but found it was turned into a nightmare by aspects of the environment. The most obvious one is who is supervising you. If you don't **fit** with how they want you to work, you will not survive. And the longer you try to work with them, the more your **confidence** will suffer.

People in my Environment

Toxic	Nutritious

The Unique You

We've finished the first section of this work book...

Well done for sticking with it... I know it is hard... boring in places... but if you have the exercises completed to your satisfaction, that is **good enough**.

And that is the point... being 'good enough' is great.

What I have tried to do is get you to look long and hard at yourself.

OK, along the way there are lots of things you will realise you are not good at... which you would love to be better at. But let me say... **concentrate** on what you are good at... **listen** to your friends who say what they **value** you for.

The objective of this section of the book is to help you clarify the answer to **Who am I?** Be happy knowing what your talents are... how you use them... what you value and what is important to you in your life in terms of those who are important for you to have around.

If you bring all the previous exercises together and look for the **themes** and the specific values and talents you have, you will start to see the 'unique you' emerging.

Don't be afraid of this because it will help you decide what it is you really **want to do** in terms of the talents you want to use, how you want to use them, in what environments and with what types of people (and I'm not talking about being a doctor or engineer here).

You might be frightened that this process limits the kind of work you fit. You are absolutely right – that you will fit certain activities and not others, but you know if you did something where you didn't fit, you would not do well and probably fail.

What you are creating is a 'me' **blueprint** for success, not failure!

What these exercises do is clarify your purpose (the kind of work you might want to do and the life you might want to live), your talents and how you use them (in the most satisfying ways), your values and how they guide how you do what you do, in the right environment.

Armed with this knowledge, the next stage is to **explore** the world of work to find out what type of work **fits** you best... so that you find the best fit for you in terms of finding a meaningful and satisfying career.

YOUR NOTES

YOUR NOTES

WHERE | *am I going?*

Where am I going?

The world out there... is pretty frightening... even if you have answered **Who am I?** from the previous exercises. Where do you start to look for a role that fits you and meets all of your requirements?

'What if...?' is something that goes through your mind quite often at this stage because you are never sure when you make a decision that it is the right one. Hopefully, the previous exercises will help enormously as they provide both a **blueprint** and **compass** to guide you through the world of work.

If you keep your blueprint and compass in mind, believe it or not... it actually doesn't matter where you start looking for that right job!

They become your rules as you go through the job search process... and they are so simple. As are the rules of career management, remember... **Who am I?**... **Where am I going?**... and **How am I going to get there?**

Turning the 'me' blueprint into the 'job' blueprint

The two rules are:

1) Stick to the blueprint you have now created based on what you have found out about yourself.

2) Keep looking until you feel... yep... this feels good... this is it... it fits... this role energises me and makes me want to get up in the morning.

DO NOT fall into the trap of doing what everyone else is doing... you will be tempted every day... as people ask:

"How many CVs have you sent off this week?"

And...

"So... how many interviews have you arranged?"

And...

"How many recruitment agencies are you registered with..?"

It is a big bad world out there and when you feel a little unsafe... **every** suggestion sounds, in the heat of the moment, a good one.

It is so easy, **SO EASY**, to start listening to all those people who think they know better.

Can I just say one thing? **THEY DON'T**. Quite simple really...

You have done your **preparation**... remember?

You have a **blueprint**... do they?

You have a **compass**... If you asked them, would they have any idea what you are talking about...

Only you know 'you' fully...

Only you know what energises you...

Only you know what you want... so don't listen to them.

Keep to your blueprint of what you want and keep **searching** until you find that job that makes you want to get up in the morning!

They will be saying to you... **"Be realistic... in this market, any job is better than no job"**...

Stick to your plan and it will pay dividends...

So we need to create **armour** against people telling us what to do...

We need to **create** a way of presenting ourselves to those we want to talk to, that is easy to understand, easy to back up and with helpful examples.

This enables us to make **connections** with people so that we can explore the different worlds of work that potentially excite us.

Literally, we need to go out as explorers did in the days when there was an **unknown**... prepared... but having no clue what to expect apart from an adventure!

Get ready to explore the world of career opportunities

So the first thing we need is... an easy way to explain who we are and what we are looking for... and **IT IS NOT A CV!**

Can we leave a CV at this moment? It's a document which is not helpful at this stage.

We want something that helps us **EXPLORE** the opportunities out there.

At this stage we are not looking for a job, we are exploring the job market and this eventually will help us find the right job.

So if people ask for a CV, you need to say that at this time you are not looking for a job... you are exploring the **opportunities** that may lead to a job.

You can add that you don't want just any job... you want one that is **right** for you...

Instead of a CV, you can offer them what I am going to suggest.

So, you need a statement that explains **Who am I?**, that unique you that you created in the last section. But for the world out there, we need a **shorthand** way of explaining it, and it is best to tell people what we do and have done... not simply roles we have held.

Everyone is addicted to that bit of paper called a CV. As you can tell, I try to wean everyone I work with off it as the main tool in their search for a job.

If you look at it, the CV is to do with the past... what roles you have held... not what you are capable of in the future, and if you have not had much experience of 'jobs', how useful is it really going to be?

In fact, the last three jobs I had... first as a management consultant... then as HR Director and lastly, Chief Executive, did not start with a CV. They all started by **gathering** information and **talking** to people so the decision to hire me was made before they saw my CV – that's your objective... because it is always the best way. If no CVs are involved, it means the employer is looking at you... not at a CV that fits a job description.

It also means the job role will be moulded around you, rather than what most people have to put up with... moulding themselves around a job that doesn't quite fit!

We are looking for that **bespoke** job, not one off the peg!!

It will be a bit like 'mission impossible' because everyone, well, almost everyone will say: **"Can I see a CV?"** I suggest saying: **"I haven't written it yet, but I do have a short description of who I am and what I do, if that would help?"**

(we'll cover the PFS in a short while...)

A CV automatically says: **"I'm looking for a job, so please interview me".**

When you are looking for a job, people you are in contact with tend to go on the defensive and they will read that piece of paper to find out why you won't be suitable.

In so many cases, it is used as a negative document because everyone uses it to find out what you haven't got!

Now at the start of your career, you **haven't got** a lot of... job **experience**...

...and if you use the CV you will have it drummed home to you how much you haven't got... great for your **confidence**, don't you think?

Also, if you use a CV at this stage, the process of exploring goes completely out of the window – people don't give you information, they ask you for it, which without doing your **exploration first** will show you to be a complete ignoramus!

You don't want to get into a conversation something like this...

Potential information giver (to whom you have made the mistake of giving a CV): **"So, why do you want to join our company?"**

You: **"Um... er... Actually, I thought that was why I was contacting you – to find out... I have done some research and I'd like to know more about the graduate training programme... particularly in relation to a role in your international research division."**

OK... I admit, I turned it round to your **advantage**... but it could have just been an **Um... er...** kind of meeting!

So, hopefully you can see being **addicted** to using your CV is a no-no until you've done your exploration and are ready to present yourself properly for a particular role or area...

Know who you are and what you want to do.

So, **shock** everyone by **NOT** producing a CV and asking for information rather than trying to get a job.

By doing this, you will stand out head and shoulders above everyone else... at least, you will be remembered... and respected... which is no bad thing!

The more I think about it, the more I believe it is about not **panicking**. If you have done the exercises, have learned to be a little more detached, you will come across much stronger... you won't seem **desperate** for a job (and let me tell you, you definitely don't want to come across as desperate. Getting a job because someone feels sorry for you is not a good start to any career!)

Explaining the Unique You

So looking at your **unique you**, what is the easiest way of explaining who you are?

Let's look at some real-life examples of brief opening statements which clarify who the people are and what they do...

"I am a corporate storyteller." (Someone working in public relations who protects the reputation of organisations.)

"I enjoy solving complex people issues in large multinationals." (Someone who is an internal facilitator linked to the human resources department of a large corporation.)

"I analyse problems and identify innovative ways to turn them into positive solutions." (A student straight out of university who can draw on many examples from her past at school, from outside school activities, and part time jobs.)

"I enjoy creating financial models that simplify processes." (Someone who found a job in a bank that wasn't as boring as others had told him it would be.)

"I sell creative ideas to organisations to help them sell their products." (A university student who had looked at the world of media and found his niche as an account executive for an advertising agency.)

So, it is a bit like what is called the **elevator pitch** when the person you want to talk to is only available for a minute (as in a lift)... what can you say in a minute and keep his/her attention?

The 'strap line' **must** be something that fits you... that you feel happy to talk about as a 'way in' to any conversation where the question, "And what do you do?" comes up.

Naturally, you will need to back up this statement with some other words that help you add some 'meat to the bones' of what you have said.

Initially your pitch does not need to be perfect, it just needs to **resonate** with you enough that you don't stutter (those 'ums...' and 'ers...') when you say it! It can change as your journey of exploration continues... as you learn more about the world of work in relation to what you do and don't want to do.

Backing it up normally continues with something like **"I (am a)... which uses my key talents of (a), (b) and (c)... and I'm potentially interested in finding out more about (X) market/organisational role..."**

The reason you need this strap line is to get people to **open up** a line of communication with you... to get someone interested in you...

...and to give you useful **information**.

SWOT Analysis

It would be useful at this stage to use a **tried** and trusted tool (devised by management consultant Albert Humphrey) to examine yourself in the wider context of the world of work.

You are not necessarily at the stage of knowing the market you want to explore and focusing down on what you need to do to be seen as a credible candidate for a particular role... however, it is useful at this stage, and intermittently from now on, to use SWOT analysis to **check out** where you are.

SWOT stands for Strengths, Weaknesses, Opportunities and Threats. It is **useful** to consider them in turn and write down what they are at appropriate times on your journey to finding that right job. It's useful to repeat the exercise even when you have a job, because even the best job for you at any moment in time will still have opportunities that you may choose to take... and threats to your **progress** if you don't take the right opportunities!

You may get a déjà vu feeling doing this. Yes, you are right… it is very similar to the Good at/Enjoy doing grid… and you can even overlay the Good at/Enjoy doing grid with it. Strengths over the box 'good at and enjoy'… weaknesses over 'good at, don't enjoy'… threats over 'bad at, don't enjoy'… and opportunities over 'bad at, enjoy doing'.

The difference is that SWOT analysis looks at us from a **detached** point of view…from outside ourselves within the **context** of the world of work. We are checking from our limited experience (and possibly checking with others!) how our self exploration is linking into the context of our lives in the world.

We need to be aware, however, that when speaking to others, anything that we are looking at that is in any way considered **different** will, more often than not, be greeted by others as a risky strategy! And what I am proposing will be for many too **risky** a strategy anyway – they will try to convince you to go back to what we have said is the 'old' way of looking for a job.

I'm not going to say any more about the SWOT analysis… there is plenty of information you can get off the internet and in management books.

But, having mentioned risky strategies… here is the next one!

Your Present and Future Statement

We talked earlier about the unique you... and the fact that a CV's weakness is that it is about the past and is a signal that you want a job.

What you need is a document that does not talk about the past in the way a CV does. You need a document that talks about what you can do in the **future**, drawing on what you have **learned from the past**.

You need a document that I call a **PFS**... a **Present and Future Statement** of what you are capable of... which covers what you might say to anyone about what you do... what you have done... and where your interest lies.

It should be no more than half a page of A4... I prefer to look at it as something I might bother to read if it was e-mailed to me and I didn't have to download it. If only for that reason, it has to be relatively short.

Example PFS

Theresa Coulter
Flat 5, 36 Cooper Rd
London
SW18 2XF
07865 994562
theresacoulter5@hotmail.com

A marketing expert who overcomes limiting beliefs around brands, businesses and people to achieve maximum performance from them.

Theresa loves a problem. What is a crisis to many is an opportunity to her. She finds few things more satisfying than taking a brand or portfolio that is in its infancy, broken or stagnating and rebuilding it into a successful profitable business. She actually likes working on those brands that others can't be talked into taking on.

Theresa believes the key to good marketing is keeping it simple. If you can't explain your marketing strategy to a 12-year-old, it probably isn't going to work. In her view, the absolute key to a successful marketing strategy is a deep and thorough understanding of the consumer. If her marketing budget was £1, she would spend it on buying one of her consumers a cup of coffee and hearing what they had to say (well, maybe she needs £2!).

Theresa's glass is always half full. She is not overly concerned by convention, but is realistic about corporate culture. She prides herself on balancing her passion for the consumer with the need to drive profitability. She has successfully applied these beliefs over 17 years of marketing experience in a wide range of industries. She has a wealth of experience across areas such as marketing strategy and planning, brand positioning development and communications strategy gained at businesses such as Gap, Unilever, Kraft Foods and Mattel Toys.

Her most recent role was as the Marketing Manager for the Kraft food business. When she left Kraft, she had more than doubled the size of the Philadelphia brand.

Theresa has a Bachelor of Economics degree, a Bachelor of Marketing degree with First Class Honours and a Diploma in Marketing Research. She is about to start her first course in NLP.

Theresa is direct and down to earth with a fun approach to work, whilst never taking her eye off the need for results.

She is interested in exploring self-employment as an option moving forward.

As you can see from the example, a PFS has a **strap line** of what you do... backed up by your talents then, depending on what you are interested in, a piece that shows you have done a little homework or achieved something.

This example PFS is of someone who is quite senior and has a lot of experience. If you don't have any work experience, you can use what you have excelled in at school or in your leisure pursuits... and can include in the document the areas where you want further information, as in the next example.

Deanne Shooter
21 Ranger's Line
Luton
LA1 2YB
shooterdeanne@hotmail.com
07922 994562

An organiser of projects and people

I am exploring opportunities to work in-house in the Recruitment/Human Resources area combining my people management skills and my interest in business.

I am at my best when working with people, acting as a catalyst for both organisations and individuals to achieve a positive outcome in difficult and complex situations.

My experience in a number of activities at university and organising a sponsored walk for a local hospice has shown me that I have an ability to take control of situations and the determination to ensure their success.

My background in finance gives me a logical and pragmatic approach to business solutions which, with my work experience over four months for a recruitment company, has confirmed my interest and intent to work in Human Resources.

My commitment to a successful career in this field has culminated in my determination to study part time for an MSc in Human Resource Management with the Open University so I can fit the studying around any job that I find is suitable.

My 2.2 degree in Business Finance from Durham University has given me a strong understanding of how markets work in theory and in practice, and how markets in financial assets operate and how they affect our daily lives.

My preference is to find a Human Resources Trainee role in a global financial company based within Central London.

WHERE AM I GOING?

This example is one of a recent graduate who has only worked for five months with a recruitment agency in London. She has understood that her key talent is organising projects and people. Her PFS gives snippets of information as tasters to entice the reader to respond.

By doing this, the person reading it can get a good idea of who you are... get a **flavour** of you... what talents you want to use... and will understand what information you want from them.

With a PFS, there is no **agenda** (hidden or open) of actually asking for a job. It might ask for information about an area and so allow the person reading it to be able to give information, but it steers well clear of talking about potential/possibilities of a job.

The objective in the exploration stage is categorically not to sell yourself (I hear a huge sigh of relief from at least 75% of you – who **hate** the idea of selling yourself!)

So what have we done so far?

We've understood we mustn't do what everyone else does...

that we shouldn't rush off with a CV to recruiters or employers...

that we must look at our **unique self** and compose a strap line that sits comfortably with us with some supporting information about our talents and why we want more information.

You must bring all the information that answers 'who am I?' into a **PFS** which clarifies who you are, what you do and what you want to **explore**.

Because our objective is to gather information, there is less pressure on us to sell ourselves... so we do it naturally by being genuinely interested in **finding out more** about our area of interest (what a person in such a role does, what talents and skills are needed for such a role... and so on).

So we get out of talking about ourselves as soon as possible when we have a discussion with someone either face to face (preferably) or on the telephone. We gather useful information... and very likely other **contacts** too, from the person we are talking to (because most people like to be helpful).

Actually what is it that are we doing?

Building relationships and a network of useful contacts that we can go back to for help when appropriate... isn't that better than sending out CVs and getting rejection letters?

Using our contacts

At this point, we need to be more **organised** – specifically in terms of our contacts. Everyone talks about 'networking' and the importance of it. We cannot get away from it – it is a fact that networking is not just extremely important, but **vital**!

In the job market, networking accounts for two-thirds of all jobs found. It is often referred to as the 'hidden' job market i.e. all the jobs that are not advertised in some way.

For us, this is very important because jobs in this hidden market are much more **flexible** – often because they have not been 'set' with a clear job description and person specification... which is great news!

Jobs in this market are like going to a tailor and having a **bespoke** suit made for you, rather than buying ready-made.

Without having job descriptions and person specifications 'set', jobs in this market tend to 'fit' much better because they evolve in a tailor-made way from a situation where a discussion of your **unique** talents leads to the person you are talking to thinking: 'I want this person to work for my company... they've got what it takes and can add real value.'

In other words, the job is made for **you**... you don't have to slot into a job that doesn't quite fit.

Too many people suffer from what I call 'ugly sister syndrome' – they have to look at jobs and ask themselves: "How can I squeeze myself into that job?"... just like the ugly sisters tried to shoehorn one foot into Cinderella's slipper. This is never a good start to any potential career!

So, can you see that if networks are important in finding jobs that are moulded to you, how important it is to develop your own **network** as soon as possible and ensure people know who you are, what you do and what you are looking for?

The good news is that any network **starts** with just one person... probably someone you already know. The objective is NOT to get a job... it is to build **relationships** with other people that may potentially be useful to you (and also them, once you are established).

People respond so much better to others who are authentic, genuinely interested, open and honest.

I'm not just saying this... it is true!

Don't fall into the trap of forcing a network because you have been told to build one (some people even compete with others as to how many networking contacts they have). Quantity isn't the point of a network... it is the **quality** of the relationships built that counts.

So, if we have only one friend in the whole world, no brothers/sisters/parents/relations, just this one person, we will say to them something like:

"I'm exploring the market to find a job which I will be good at and enjoy... I want to talk to people who are in work to understand what they do and what talents they need... I'm really interested in xxxx... that's why I really wanted to talk to you... What do you do in your job?... What do your friends do?"

"Oh! That is interesting you just mentioned xxxxx... Would you know anyone who could give me some more information on that?... Would it be possible for me to have a short conversation with them?"

...and you are on your way!

It is **simple**... OK...it might not work out quite like I said. Initially you might find it embarrassing, uncomfortable, but hey, anything you do for the first time is like this!

The hardest step is always the first one...

Now I know what goes through people's heads...

'Well, it's OK for 'x'. He/she could do that, but I just can't...'

I'm sorry, but I have to say... Bull***t... you're just being a bit of a coward... IT WORKS! So you need to get **comfortable** doing it.

Networking is one of the most important things you need to learn/cultivate/extend in your life because it acts as a huge **safety** net in so many different ways... and the sooner you **start**, the better.

So start **now**...

...and be 'anal' about it, put everyone you meet and have a decent conversation with in your 'Outlook' **contacts** – and make sure you do. It will be invaluable...

I'll stop now, but if you don't do this, forget reading the rest of this book as it won't help... I'm warning you and won't now say another word... it's up to you.

Actually, you already have a network on your social networking site – **Facebook** seems to be the biggest one and MySpace isn't far behind. From a career point of view, the best networking site to use is **LinkedIn**. Why? Because apart from its being used by many recruiters as a **source of candidates** (it is used to gather information), there are 'groups' for many interest areas and people are extremely willing to talk online. You will find you are already prepared to fill in the **profile** from your PFS!

This leads us neatly into the next section...

A little bit of research – clues along the way

So you've had a **really** interesting chat with your one friend and she has given you two other people to talk to... **FANTASTIC**, you are on your way to finding the right job for you.

Before you make a fool of yourself talking to anyone, PLEASE do just a little **initial** research on the internet!

When I was the HR Director of Ogilvy's, the advertising agency, I saw too many people who looked blankly when I asked which areas of advertising particularly interested them!

If you're not interested enough to know something before you see a contact – DON'T BOTHER. You will say: "that was **useless**", but actually... you were!!

Getting the right job is all about gathering information.

You will look at sites on the internet... talk to mates about specific areas... find people who might know people who work in those areas... speak to them... and along the way, your interest will either increase or wane... so you just follow your interest.

You will talk to people... remember things that are important to you... speak to people you will think were really helpful and some that were not (that's life). You'll check things out... and **check** again... but what keeps you going is that something about an area of work...the people in it... the environment you might work in... the use of your talents... and, most importantly, your **fascination** for work that sounds interesting... and away you go!

So, I'm saying that some conversations will be **deadly** boring, and you'll lose the will to live, but just like every **explorer**, we will find dead ends, places we don't want to go, swamps, quicksand etc... It is just part of the exploration process... and yes, it does take time. But boy, is it useful!

Why? Because, along the journey, you will:

1) Gain **confidence** in talking about yourself

2) Learn about **listening** properly

3) Learn properly what **excites** you (and what doesn't)

4) Pick up 'business' **language**... every area of work has its own language

5) Pick up the **issues** that people are grappling with in their market. Every market has its own issues and you need to know what they are because employers want to talk to candidates on the same wavelength i.e people who speak knowingly about the same issues and in their particular business language.

6) Attract employers in your market to you, because of your accumulation of the above five points. Basically, the more you **know**, the more people want to employ you. And if you are excited by a particular area of work, you will delve deeper into 'what's going on' in that area and that will attract people in that market to you.

If you are older and have been working in other areas of work, this process identifies exactly what your **transferable** skills are and also how valuable they are. Actually this is true for everyone - even those of you who have never worked before... you still have **talents**... you still have **values** and you combine them into a **unique you**. So if you are aware of who you are, it helps to enable you to talk effectively from your own standpoint.

We do need to remember at this point that we don't want any job — we want the right job. So for many of you, the **journey** may not be exciting all the time. The exploration may end up in the depths of the jungle for a long time, with you not knowing where you are going. Can I say here, **"GREAT!"** It is exactly what needs to happen – if everything was easy, there would be no excitement when you found yourself in the right place... and actually, you probably wouldn't know!

Being in the depth of the jungle for a while is **very** important because it attunes our senses to what it is we **really** want!

So yes, you'll get diseases (in other words, get caught up looking at something you 'think' is the right job, ignoring the fact you know it doesn't **feel** right), you'll get stuck in certain areas and, quite frankly, you may end up getting a job in an area that isn't right first time... that's OK too... as long as you have this 'fly buzzing around your head' asking "is this right?"

Sometimes, too, in your search, you'll talk to people and realise that to get the job you want, you first have to do a job you don't want – but if you look at the 'purpose' diagram, you will see it's worth doing it because it gets you to where you want to go in the end.

The first stages of exploration are all about getting as much **information** as possible- drowning yourself in **chaos** because the more complexity you surround yourself with, the more the right opportunities will 'emerge' . Conversely, the more you control what you do, the more you will lose sight of potential opportunities.

Using your experiences

During this exploration, your previous experiences will be **important**.

Remember we talked about keeping **detached** as you go through the self exploration? The same is true for the exploration of the world of work.

There will be plenty of people saying to you...**"that's really boring... I wouldn't look at that!"** or who laugh at potential options that you might mention.

The **key** is to not go on what other people think... try it out yourself... **investigate** properly before you dismiss a potential area of work.

It's very easy to say **"banking is boring"** without knowing a thing about it!

Your **own** experience is what is important.

If you look back on what you have experienced so far in your life, there will be lots of **clues** as to the right way to go next.

You might have worked in a bar/restaurant/shop while at school or university. This is experience that will give you lots of useful information in terms of what **abilities** you and others have **recognised** in the work you have done.

You will also have found out which types of work you find boring and which have come **easily** to you and that you have enjoyed.

If nothing else, you will know in an **organised** work environment what you like/don't like. Looking at how others work, and what they do, will also add to your information-gathering on what things you might enjoy doing.

Friends and family will give **suggestions** from their own experience of you, what **talents** they believe you have and what areas might be worth exploring to **exploit** them... but don't take what other people say as the truth... only if you truly think they are **right** for you (I see too many people whose parents are living their lives over again through their children).

It is **your** life... and as far as I'm concerned, it is the only life you lead... so live it **well**!

If it helps, create a 'temperature chart' in terms of the meetings you have. Give each meeting **marks** out of 10 in terms of how you feel about a particular job or job area. Be careful not to be **swayed** simply by how you got on with the person you saw (it is useful to at least jot down a few notes after every meeting as by the next day you will have forgotten 80% of what was said!)

I know it needs a bit of **discipline** but it is worth it... after all, you want a job that will be right for you!

You might also write **more** notes to come back to later in terms of how your blueprint **overlaps** what you got out of the meeting.

I realise I haven't said something very important which I should have said earlier: we **all** suffer from negative perceptions with no **real** basis for them, so it is very easy to speak to one person who is very negative about their job/company or area of work. Don't accept it as a truth. **ALWAYS** check with someone else before you make a decision based on **one** conversation about a particular type of work.

The same can be true the other way – someone really **enthuses** about an area that 'sounds' good, that 'pays really well'... then you have to look at it with a detective's eye – why is it so good?

Often, those jobs that look good initially run out of steam very quickly. In other words, they have no **longevity**. You end up in a cul-de-sac... the job doesn't lead anywhere.

Unfortunately, it is true to say, the **best** jobs often pay reasonably badly initially... but that is because of something called 'supply and demand' (you might have learned this at school or university!) In other words, because everyone can see the job is good, the employer doesn't need to pay high wages to **attract** people.

So, here you are, in the midst of exploring the job market, having had good and bad experiences of meetings. You've got an understanding of a few fields of work... you've decided that engineering isn't for you, or that in nursing there is too much blood... and it is embarrassing, fainting all the time!

But you have found that banking isn't as bad as it sounds and there are some really **interesting** jobs there... just as many as are in the construction world, particularly the design end... and it would be good to get into advertising, but there are a lot of people who are much more **committed** than you... and the starting pay is **really** bad!

These are the kind of thoughts that might go through your head after some initial exploration... the information you have gathered might not have led to a **definite** job area... but you have found out that there is something about a creative environment that attracts you...but you are not committed to advertising enough to throw yourself into it... you liked the design elements in the construction industry but that marketing department in the bank was really interesting...

So what is going on?

You are **thinking** why you liked certain jobs and not others... looking back on your **past**, you might realise you like structure around your creativity... you were best when a project was given to you and you added some creative flair rather than came up with a creative idea.

So you will be analysing opportunities based on what you have **learned** regarding **Who am I?**

However, you will also be guided by how you feel. At the end of the day, all the logic in the world about the 'best' job will disappear into insignificance if the area doesn't **feel** right for you!

As your journey continues and the exploration gets more focused on certain areas that **attract** you, you will get deeper into the markets that **interest** you and want to get more information. As your interest and **enthusiasm** for a particular area grows, so does your **knowledge** and as your knowledge grows, you are able to talk the 'language' of that area of work. And as people **engage** more with you because 'you are like them', your **confidence** will grow... And as it grows, you will come across better and seem more **employable**... that's the theory... and it actually happens in practice!!

At this stage you will be in the **top** 10% of the normal distribution curve of those seeking work in that area....a really good place to be!!

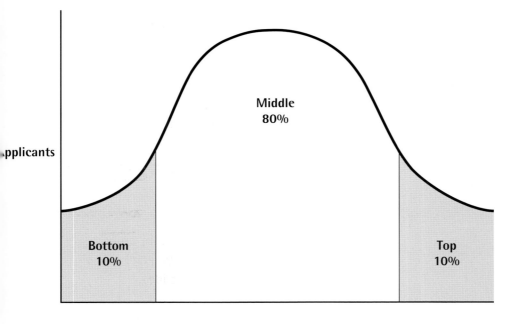

Degree of 'fit' to the job

The thing you can be truly proud of is that you are in **control** of your career. You are finding out about the world of work that is of interest to you, you are not reliant on anyone advising you what to do, because you have something that 90% don't have – **knowledge** – knowledge of the big bad world out there – knowledge of what is going on and what the issues are that each job sector is facing. You are also getting **clearer** about what it is you want to concentrate on, in terms of particular sectors and roles within them. The trick is not to decide too quickly, and when you are in exploration mode that should be **all** you are doing. If people along the way start interviewing you, I would suggest saying "can I get back to you once I have finished my research?" Yes, I know I'm **mad** to say this. But you have to be a little mad to get what you truly **want**!

All I can tell you is, if you say that you need more time for research, you will not only shock the person who has offered you an interview or a job, they will also be impressed by you at the same time.

Only when you really **think** and **feel** 'this is somewhere I could really do something I will enjoy and succeed in' should you make that **decision**... and that's in the next section with that thing we haven't talked about that much... now... what was it?... Oh yes... the CV!

YOUR NOTES

YOUR NOTES

HOW am I going to get there?

How am I going to get there?

So, you have **found** out about who you are, and you have also **explored** the job market to find out what you want to do using a strap line with some supporting statements about your talents.

You have gathered lots of **information** about the world of work and have built and extended your network of contacts. So let's make things even more complicated, and I hope you have already done so... by looking beyond where you have got to.

I'm writing this in the South of France. And I have just seen a client who lives here part of the time... yet he has just got a job in the UK. He is off to see friends in South Africa for a short holiday and is looking at completing on a property deal in Thailand.

This kind of **life** is becoming quite normal.

The world is shrinking... and many of us have international contacts and potentially **international** jobs... and other 'bits' of work on the side.

Some people, like me, have **portfolio** careers, spending time on different projects sometimes quite different from each other... so many of us are in **contact** with colleagues and clients all around the globe on a daily basis. I, for instance, have just come off a conference call organised by my client in Singapore and linked in with India, Australia and the United States.

So, what I am saying is that you need to set your sights as **high** as you want to go because you are working in a global market place – not just the UK or Europe... so think about the areas you are exploring... are you exploring **widely** enough?... and I mean this in every sense, but particularly geographically. What stops you, for instance, completing your degree in another country?... Thousands now do. What stops you exploring your lines of enquiry within Europe... or talking to companies you are interested in joining about **opportunities** elsewhere in the world?

When you start **reaching** out beyond your locality, your country and

beyond, it makes it even more important that you stand out from the crowd and are clear about what you want, because instead of **competing** with thousands, you are now competing with millions!

It is even more important to have information at your fingertips and to be **visible** across the globe. So, **where** do you want to work?

Where... from the point of view of location... sector... organisation... department? What **extra** research does this entail? You may need to beef up your **contacts** through the internet, through Facebook, YouTube, Twitter, and definitely through business networks – LinkedIn and Plaxo.

Start to look **broader**. Even if you want to remain in your home town, you still need to understand how the sector you are looking at is developing nationally and internationally... if nothing else, because it will **impress** the person who will interview you!

As I said earlier, 50% of **jobs** today did not exist 20 years ago. You don't want to start a career in one of those areas that is on the decline... with no way of transferring to a sector which is growing.

You can find so much information on the **internet**. But remember that whatever you do, you need both generalist and specialist skills in your chosen line of work linked to your talents and values.

One thing to bear in mind in relation to my point about how jobs have changed... We can forget that those people we are seeking **advice** from in relation to finding that 'right' career may not be as **aware** of the changes in the world of work as they should.

I often hear people of my own age talking about their son or daughter getting a **proper** job like banking... accountancy... etc. They do not see, for example, the huge expansion in the **communications** industry as offering 'proper' jobs... yet in terms of what I said about new and growing jobs... this industry has grown enormously over the last 20 years and is continuing to grow... so be aware that there are new jobs being created all the time by the advances in **technology** and how it is used.

What are you going to say?

Now we have to bring together all the information from sections A and B into a way of talking about yourself that is both **powerful** and above all, **authentic**.

Looking back on what you have learned both about yourself, and the areas of interest to you, what examples of how you have used your talents have become more relevant to the type of work you want to do? From your investigations in the world of interest to you, what **examples** from your life so far are useful to talk about?

What you need is **short stories** that help to **support** your case for potential employment having understood the area you want to work in and where you have **contacts** you can go back to.

By this stage you should **know** the market you are interested in pretty well.

By that I mean: you know the key **players**; the up and coming competitors; the innovators in the market place; the **issues** in terms of the threats and potential opportunities (I'm assuming that you have already read section B and thought about each sector from the **SWOT** point of view – strengths and weaknesses, opportunities and threats); the specific area you are interested in; your likely **progression** from an entry point to one which suits your 'aims' and 'purpose' (remember that? It is **really** important).

So, from this, decide on the 'stories' that show how you could potentially add value. If you are at the start of your job search and career, you may not have specific 'work experience' to go on, but you will certainly have examples which show how you have approached an event or issue and how you dealt with it. You will have **examples** of selling yourself... negotiating... working in a team... coming up with new ideas, and so on. In fact, you will be able to show examples in the same way anyone who has had work experience can... so don't beat yourself up if you haven't got it! Decide on what stories you need to cover off most of the questions a

Use your own qualities to prepare *your* story about yourself

potential interviewer may have – and also be aware of the areas, that you may need to admit to, where you have no experience (although there are **always** experiences from your past that would give **hints** as to how you would behave in similar situations).

It is now time to go back to those contacts to see what their view is in terms of what to look for in terms of a role in that area. Of course, it is not the examples of stories alone that you have to offer – the fact you have explored the market well (if not thoroughly!), will help you to **stand out** from the crowd.

Your approach should still be one of **seeking** advice – but now it is more specific in terms of potential opportunities for employment. At no point must you put any of your contacts under any pressure to 'do' anything for you. It is important for two reasons: one, that the fact they are giving you their **time** and **information** is enough; second is more important to you... **you** need to keep in control. If someone is contacting someone else on your behalf, what are they saying? Even if you have been very **clear** about who you are and what you do, you have immediately lost **control** of the situation – much better to speak to the person yourself, stating your contact suggested you do so!

OK, in lots of cases things may not go according to **plan** - but if you can, try to keep in control of every contact. It really helps to keep the messages you are putting out clear and **consistent**.

The CV

At this stage, you will need to have a CV ready just in case you need to produce it. As I have said before, don't produce it at the drop of a hat... try to avoid sending it to anyone until you have gathered all the information you need to feel really confident and you have already had contact with them in person, or at least by telephone.

In my view, a CV should just **back up** what you have already said and reflect the information you have gained... be written in the **right language** considering the talents and skills that are required and therefore it should include achievements that really stand out and confirm you are the **right person** for the job!... I don't believe a CV should act as an introduction, which I'm sure many would disagree with!

Let's face it... if you are just starting out, work experience will be sparse, and even if there are good companies on your CV, did you get them under your own steam or was it through your parents' networks... what does that say about you – both good and bad?

A CV just tells people what someone has done in the past and not what they are **capable** of doing in the future (For more information on putting your CV together, please see Recommended reading: *The Career Repair Kit*).

However you can help yourself and a reader/interviewer if you put enough 'hooks' in it...

HOOKS

Hooks are very important to **catch** the interviewer and put him/her in a place where they ask the right questions. In other words hooks are embedded in what you say about yourself and are always found in your 'achievements'.

Here, I must say that a CV without achievements is worse than useless. No one will give it a second glance.

For how long do you think someone looks at your CV? I would say 2-3 seconds at a first glance. And unless there is something that hooks him/her into reading a bit more, that is all you will get - a cursory glance and straight into the bin!

So we need to work from a very old acronym —**AIDA** (Strong 1925[6])— that reminds us of the four stages of the sales process. AIDA stands for:

Attract – you've got to have something that will capture someone's 'attention'... a good way is to surprise them by doing something slightly different (no, it doesn't mean writing your CV on orange paper!)

Interest – as the person reads what you say, there are other attraction points that maintain or heighten the person's interest in reading further.

Desire - you need enough points of attraction and interest to lead to a point where the reader wants to 'know more'. That 'know more' is the whole point of a CV. Its sole purpose is to get the reader to want to see you, or speak to you.

Lastly there is **Action** and believe it or not, I have seen literally hundreds of CVs without any contact details!

You need your mobile number and an email address as **priorities**, with your postal address (often not used nowadays!) as a backup.

So, if you take this literally, your CV must be **short**, easy to scan in 2-3 seconds and have enough hooks in it to get the person to pick up the phone or email you.

If you follow this advice, the CV does one crucial thing - it adds **credibility** to what contact you have already made by confirming what you have said in person.

So don't give a life history over seven pages... (yes, I have seen them referring to being one of the three kings in the Christmas play at the age of six!)

If you know yourself, and what the market you are **interested** in is looking for, you won't go too far wrong.

It is my experience that the majority of people take the job that seems to suit them best from the interviews they have attended – often based, in reality, on liking the interviewer and feeling that in some way there is a supportive environment, or the prospect of making money (which they feel will impress friends and family).

But was it the **right choice** and could they have done something to make themselves feel **happier** about the choice they made? This is why it is so important to create the 'blueprint' from the exercises you did looking at "Who am I?"

Pre-interview

So, you have got to the point of a formal interview... and I hope it is not one where you have been sent a job description and person specification (that old ugly sister syndrome!). Hopefully, there is little information on the job so the discussion is about **you** and what you can bring to the organisation rather than looking at a tight job role and checking if you can fit it. If the former is true, and they are looking at you specifically from how you fit the job, don't worry about it!

If there is a job description, remember don't be an 'ugly sister' by trying to shoehorn yourself into the job. You **must be yourself**, talk about your talents and, if the interviewer asks about talents you don't have or don't want to use, be honest. **Don't pretend** to be something you are not. Even if you were able to hoodwink the interviewer, what will happen if you are offered the job?... You will be found out, or have to put all your energy into evading being found out. Forget it... it's not worth it!

You will need to do your **homework** on the organisation you are going to see. It is useful to talk to your existing contacts in the area for their opinion plus look at their annual **report and accounts** (if they are published) which can tell you what has been happening in the past year or two... and, hopefully, how the organisation is growing (or contracting...).

Do a search on the internet to see if there has been any positive or negative **press** comments... all information you collect helps you to feel more in control at the interview.

It certainly sounds impressive if you have bothered to find out some of the key issues the company is facing and have a view about them.... And, importantly, this kind of **information** can help you to leave a positive last **impression** when answering the often dreaded question: "Have you any further questions?"

UCTs

Your 'unique combination of talents' should be very **clear** in your mind prior to any interview. (Yes... we've had PFSs, now it's UCTs!)

By now, through your desk research and the conversations you have had with people when exploring your areas of interest.... you should have a good idea of what you can **offer** and how you can stand out from the crowd in any interview you attend.

You must work out how you **fit** the organisation, from specific information you have gleaned, before the interview.

For example, you must **prepare** yourself in relation to any recent issues that the organisation has been dealing with – how would your talents help with these?

Have you looked at your 'stories' and tried them out with friends to get them fresh in your mind? Which ones are most **relevant** to that particular interview?

Get your friends to comment on how you come across... how clearly your talents come across... are the stories relevant... too short... too long ... not talking about 'we' but rather what **I** did.

Remember that whatever you do in the interview, do not try to be something you are not, authenticity is important... No! **Critical**!

The interview

Be clear what your objectives are **before** you go for an interview.

What do you want to know more about? What do you want to get across? What impression do you want to make?

Be clear also that interviews are about **exchanging information**; they are not about being subservient and just reacting to questions fired at you. You have to gather enough information at the interview for you to make **decisions** about whether it is the right organisation for you (refer back to your results on the environment exercise) in terms of where it is, the kind of people you will be working for and with... and the culture... is it all **conducive** to you giving of your best?

I always say that you must never 'need' a job at an interview because it comes across that you are desperate. You certainly don't think as clearly if 'the job' is the only one you are going for...

...and I can assure you that this is true from the experience of hundreds of people I have worked with over the years.

Knowing there is something else available allows you to keep the **detachment** necessary to think straight and ask the right questions... worrying that you are presenting yourself well enough when everything seems to depend on getting a particular job can disrupt your interview and technique rather than allowing them to **flow**.

Worrying about what you are saying creates a situation where all you can be is reactive. You always come across badly. OK it is important to 'want' a job enough, to be a little nervous to give you a little adrenaline before the interview – but what I'm saying is: **don't be desperate**!

A tip that is always useful:

I always take a written **list** of things I want to get out of the interview with me... the interviewer normally makes some notes, so why don't you, too?

So I tend to have a notebook of some description in front of me in the interview where I can refer to questions and make notes on the answers I have received.

If, on the other hand, the interview is 'informal' (and by the way that is NEVER the case... prepare even more for informal interviews) and the interviewer doesn't have notes and material in front of him or her, then you should **mirror** the **behaviour** – only at the end, if you think you've forgotten to mention something, should you take out your 'list' – it shows you have come prepared!

I always suggest that if nothing has been said about the **interview process** moving forward, it is important to ask what is to happen next so that you are clear about when might you hear about the next stage... and also how many **stages** there might be!

Recently a number of people have suffered very **long** interview processes where virtually everyone of any importance in the company has been involved. It bodes badly if decisions don't seem to be made quickly. I'm of the opinion that you either 'fit' or you don't. It's just down to whether they have a **budget** to pay for you – that is an issue that sometimes needs some work... and sometimes this means accepting an 'internship' or 'temp-to-permanent' position so the organisation 'tries you out' (and you, by the way, have the same opportunity if you are unsure whether the organisation is **right** for you).

More and more organisations have been using graduate 'interns' where they pay little – but the person gains experience that might help them find a job. Some companies treat their interns well, others do not! So, when analysing the **usefulness** of certain positions, be careful that you are getting something out of them... rather than being used as 'slave labour'.

Getting to interview is 50% of the way to getting a job. Normally by now, you have 'passed' the "has he/she got the skills/talents needed for the job" stage. The interview is to find out if you use them in the ways that 'fit' the organisation... and that your **attitude** and **behaviour** also fit what is needed in the role.

And for you, the same is true: you believe it looks like an organisation that will use your skills and talents well. You are going along to find out 'how' those skills and talents you have might be utilised and what the **prospects** are if you do well.

And there is one very important aspect that you should give particular consideration. Can you **get on** with the person who is to be your boss?

Whatever happens, the meeting with your prospective boss, at whatever point in the interview process, is the most important. You have to know how he/she **operates** and whether it is in a way that works with you. So many of the people I see for career counselling have been 'damaged' by ignoring the fact that their boss works in a different way, and trying to work in that way has undermined their self confidence.

There are many different ways of operating that you may find yourself under. From being totally **controlled** at every step, with no room for you to have any choice of action, through to being left working totally on your own initiative with no **direction** whatsoever. (Check your answer to the Environments Exercise.)

Along that continuum, bosses will **expect** you to work in particular ways. If you don't, they will not value you because they don't recognise the way you work as acceptable. If your boss works in a different way, and you didn't pick it up at interview, my advice is "get out quick!" before things start going horribly wrong – and they will. Don't try and stick it out – all that will happen is that you will be damaged by the experience.

Time and again I see successful young people who talk about their first boss "who was great and really **supported** me"... that's what you want... that's what is important to look out for... Who is going to support you the most and give you the confidence and the skills to really **shine**?

So, again, hopefully you can see the reason why we spend so much time understanding ourselves... without that we cannot understand others... and see how we can **operate** to our optimum in an environment conducive to OUR way of working. So many people put up with working at less than their **optimum**, by complying with working to "the way things are done around here".

Do not fall into that trap – you will become an **also ran**, a 'lemming', a worker who just does a job... and a negative person to boot!

So I think that is all I want to say about the interview – read about open/closed questions etc. elsewhere – I'm just covering those points that people don't tend to **concentrate** on but that are **vital** for your long term job satisfaction.

Comparing opportunities – your job blueprint

Oh yes... I'm assuming that you have not put all of your eggs in one basket... I've implied that having only one job on the cards is not good and talked about how you come across in interview if that is the case.

What seems to work best is to try to have at least **three opportunities** on the go at any one time.

	JOB A	JOB B	JOB C
Prospects	7	2	5
Location	3		8
Environment		8	
People		4	8
Culture	8		
Team work	8	3	3
Independence	7	2	
Salary	4		8

Points soon start to add up

If you have completed all the exercises and tasks I have mentioned here, you will not arrive at one opportunity – if anything, you will have a problem **identifying** which of quite a **selection** you may go for!

And that selection may cut across differing **sectors** because you are actually interested in more than one role in more than one area... And that is great... even though it gives you an enormous headache thinking which you would choose above others.

There is a way to **clarify** which opportunities are better than others and that is to write down on the side of one sheet of paper all the **criteria** you 'need' in a job in terms of all the elements you have discovered about yourself – so, for instance:

'At least 50% flexibility of action' might be one of your criteria **linked** to a 'supportive boss' and 'using my analytical skills' (all these, by the way, will be shorthand for what you **mean**... just like in the Good at/Enjoy doing grid where we 'unpacked' what we meant by each thing we put in that top right hand box...).

You'd add the top five **values** you have identified... and the **culture** you want, the kind of **people** you want to work with, the **environment** that is most **conducive** to you working well...

Then from your **exploration** – what were the things that **excited** you that you would want in your future? Yes, you need to think about your future as well as the present. Some jobs look great in the immediate-to-short term, but they soon peter out! Others don't look so good initially, but later on the opportunities can open up immensely!

So, write that list, as long as you can make it. Then give each of your criteria 10 points – so, if you have 10 criteria, 100 points would be the **ideal** job for you!

Now decide what would be the minimum 'fit' of job to you that you would accept... 50%, so 50?... 75%, so 75?

Then look at the opportunities **open** to you and mark them against each criterion.

It's surprising how often at least one opportunity does not even reach your 'bottom' score! You can do this quite logically... but actually what really happens is the one that **feels** better tends to get better scores all the way through!

By the way, it is useful to do this **prior** to an interview so that you clarify the areas where you can't put a figure against a criterion, or if there is a whole section that is low and therefore needs to be explored more in the interview.

So, in order to make decisions about opportunities, be clear what your **purpose** and **aims** are initially. Don't get caught up in objectives – the job that pays more so that you can get that car you want, may force you into a cul-de-sac later.

Yes... you want to enjoy the **present**... but you also need to look longer term to the **future**... Does a job open up lots of opportunities to **extend** your talents into other areas, give you opportunities to travel (if this is an interest of yours) or specialise in an area that you can't stop enjoying however much you work at it?

JBDI

Once you have made up your mind, it becomes simple 'JBDI' (Just Bl**dy Do It!)

Get on with it - start that job and make sure you **push** for everything you want. Work **hard**, but also work **smart**. Keep one eye on the job market. **Keep in touch** with all those people who helped you to this point, tell them where you are - offer help in the future - above all... **stay in touch**.

Never get into a position where you feel you have to do something that sends you down a wrong path – from now on you are in **control** of your life and your career in particular... sure, your views will change – the job market will **definitely** change - but the key is you know "who you are" and what gets you up in the morning.

NEVER forget that and you will have a great life, meet great people and have a successful career – one that you want and that no one else has decided for you.

Have a great life and really enjoy what you do – you deserve it!

You are off! Good luck!

YOUR NOTES

Recommended reading

1. *The Career Repair Kit* David Royston-Lee; downloadable via www.davidroystonlee.com

2. *Managing Your Self: Management by Detached Involvement* Parikh, Jagdish; Wiley-Blackwell, 1993 (new ed.)

3. *The Crystal-Barkley Guide To Taking Charge Of Your Career* Barkley, Nella and Sandburg, Eric; Workman Publishing, 1996

4. *Kim* Kipling, Rudyard; Penguin Popular Classics, 1994
ISBN: 978 0 14062 049 8

5. *Toward a Psychology of Being* (3rd ed.) Maslow, A., & Lowery, R. (Ed.); New York: Wiley & Sons (1998)

6. *Theories of Selling* Strong, E. C. (1925); Journal of Applied Psychology, 9: 75-86

The Johari window, a graphic model of interpersonal awareness, Proceedings of the Western Training Laboratory in Group Development (Los Angeles: UCLA) Luft, Joseph; Ingham H (1955)

Flow – The Classic Work on How to Achieve Happiness Csikszentmihalyi, Mihaly; Rider & Co, 2002 (revised ed.)

YOUR NOTES

List of exercises and diagrams

LIST OF EXERCISES AND DIAGRAMS

List of cartoons

YOUR NOTES

YOUR NOTES